Poco Ponies

Colorare

Coloring Pages for Kids

Coloring Pages for Kids
An imprint of Ciparum LLC

Poco Ponies Colorare
© 2017 Ciparum LLC
All rights reserved.
ISBN-10:1-63589-408-5
ISBN-13:978-1-63589-408-0

Coloring Pages for Kids

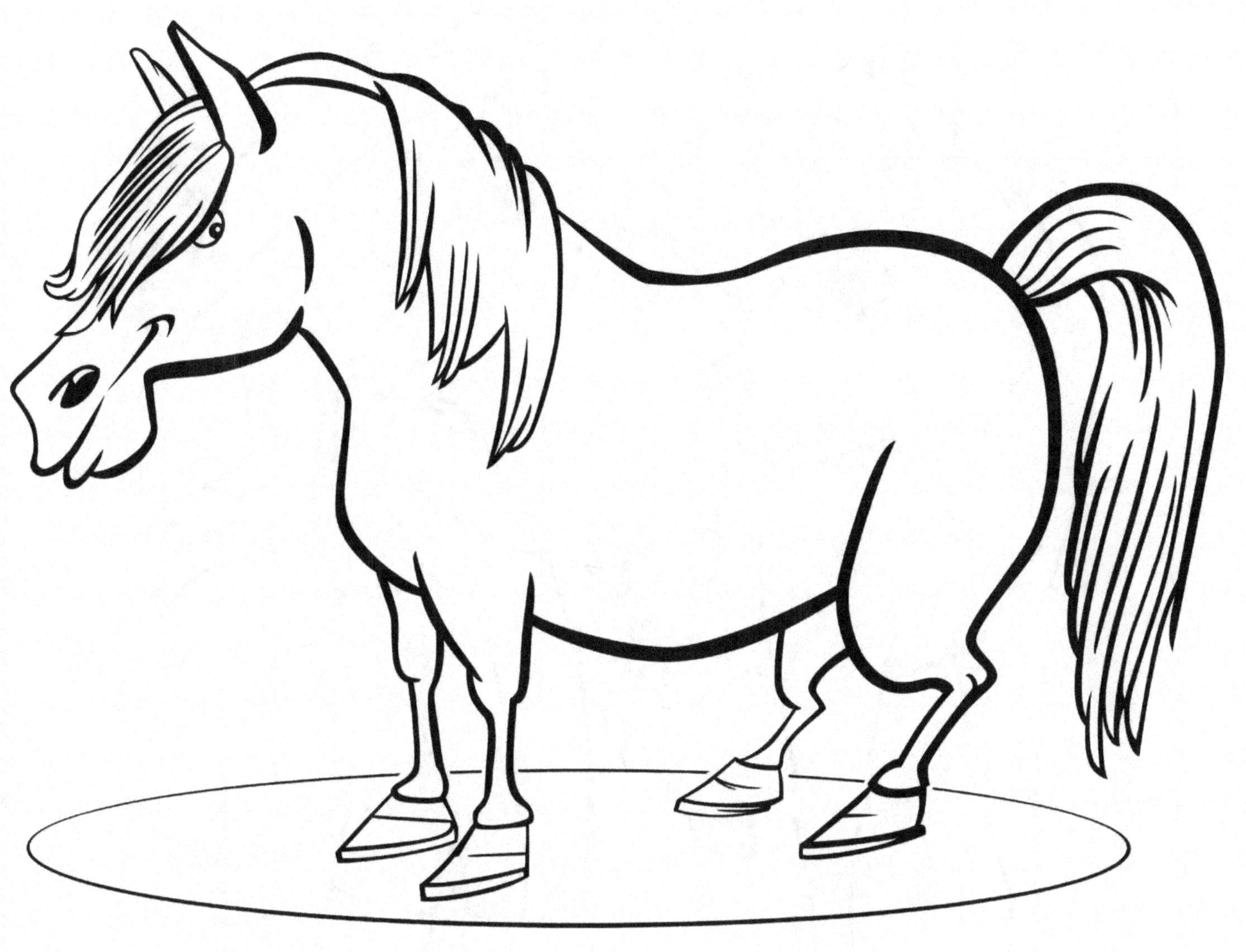

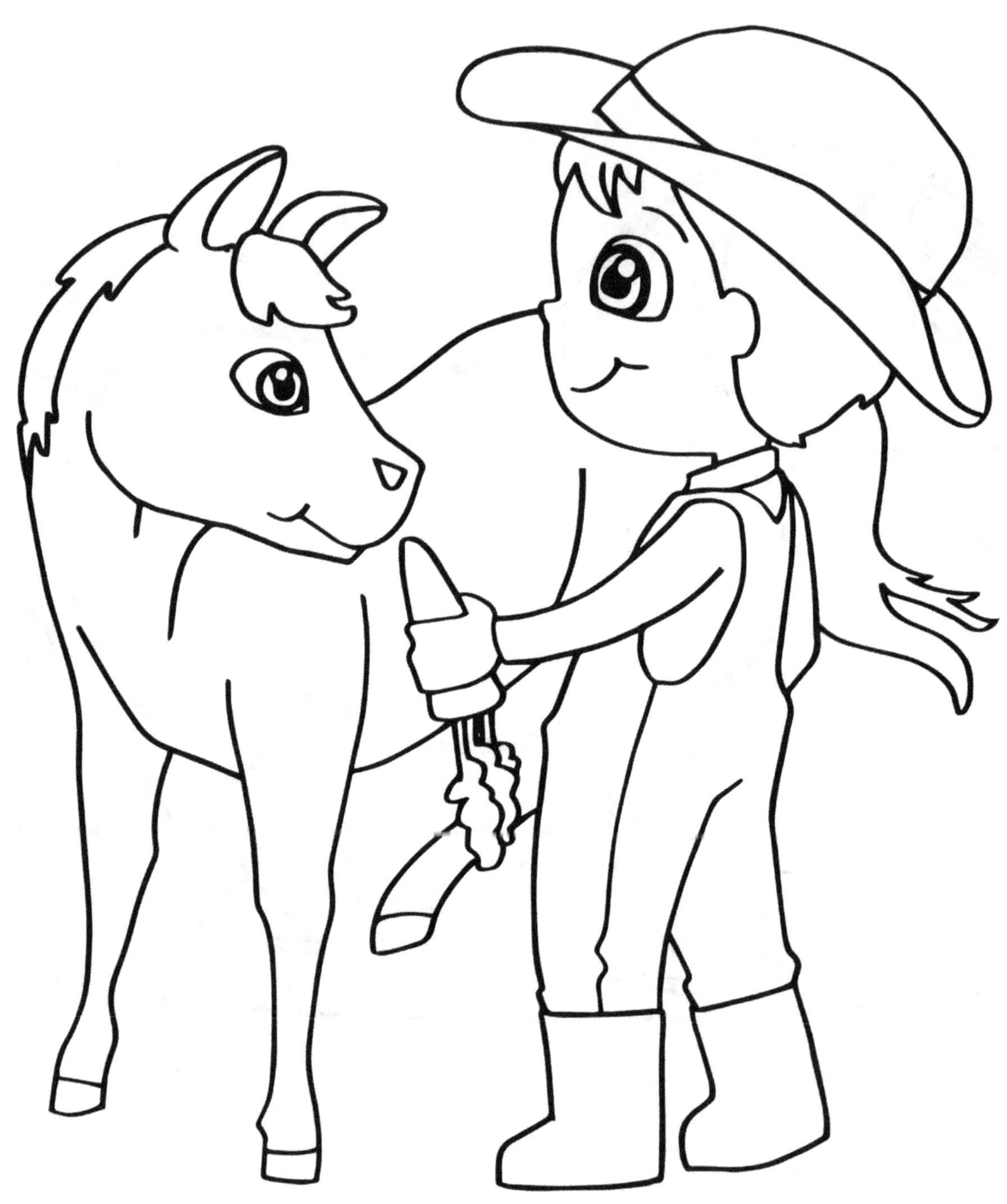

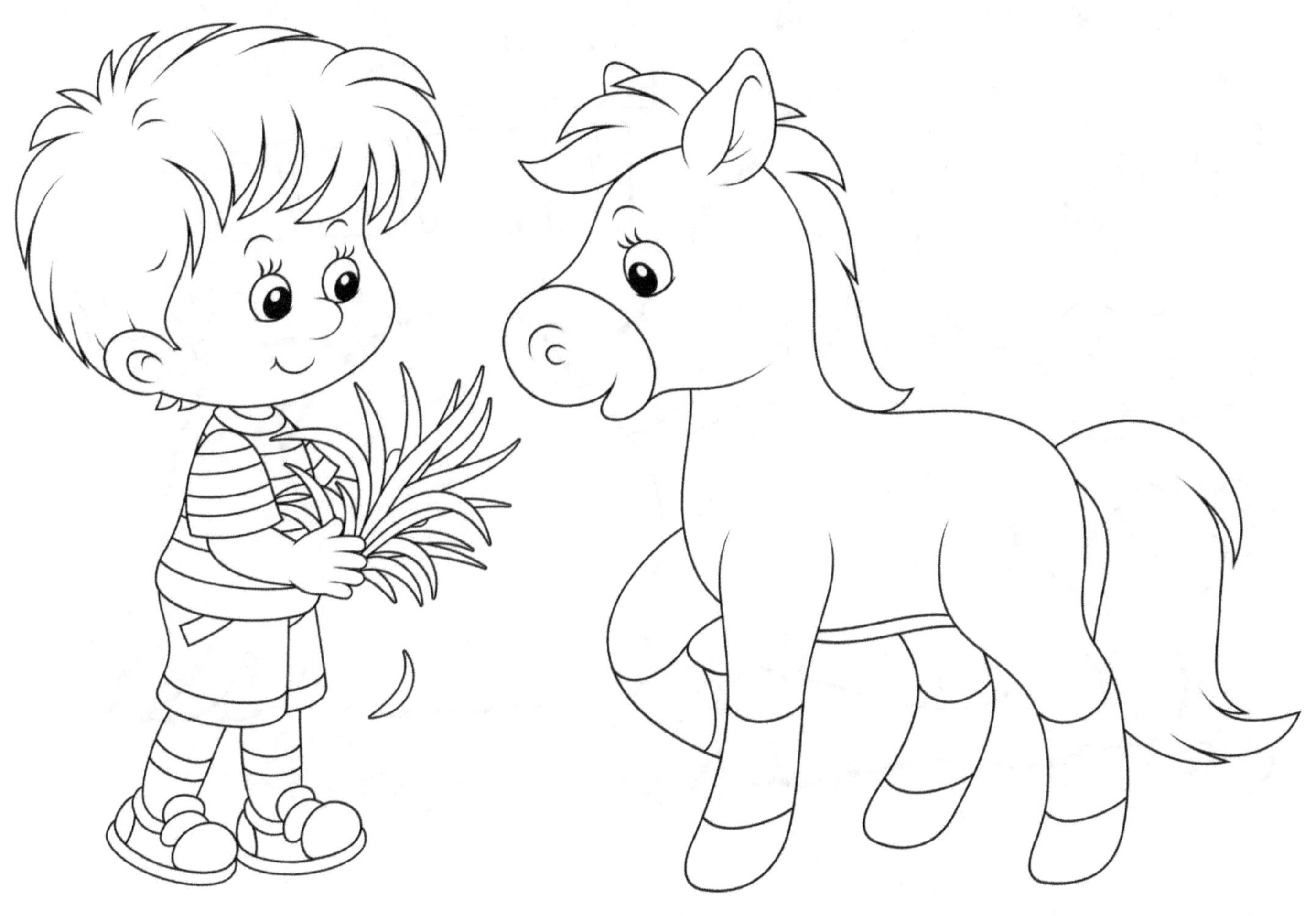

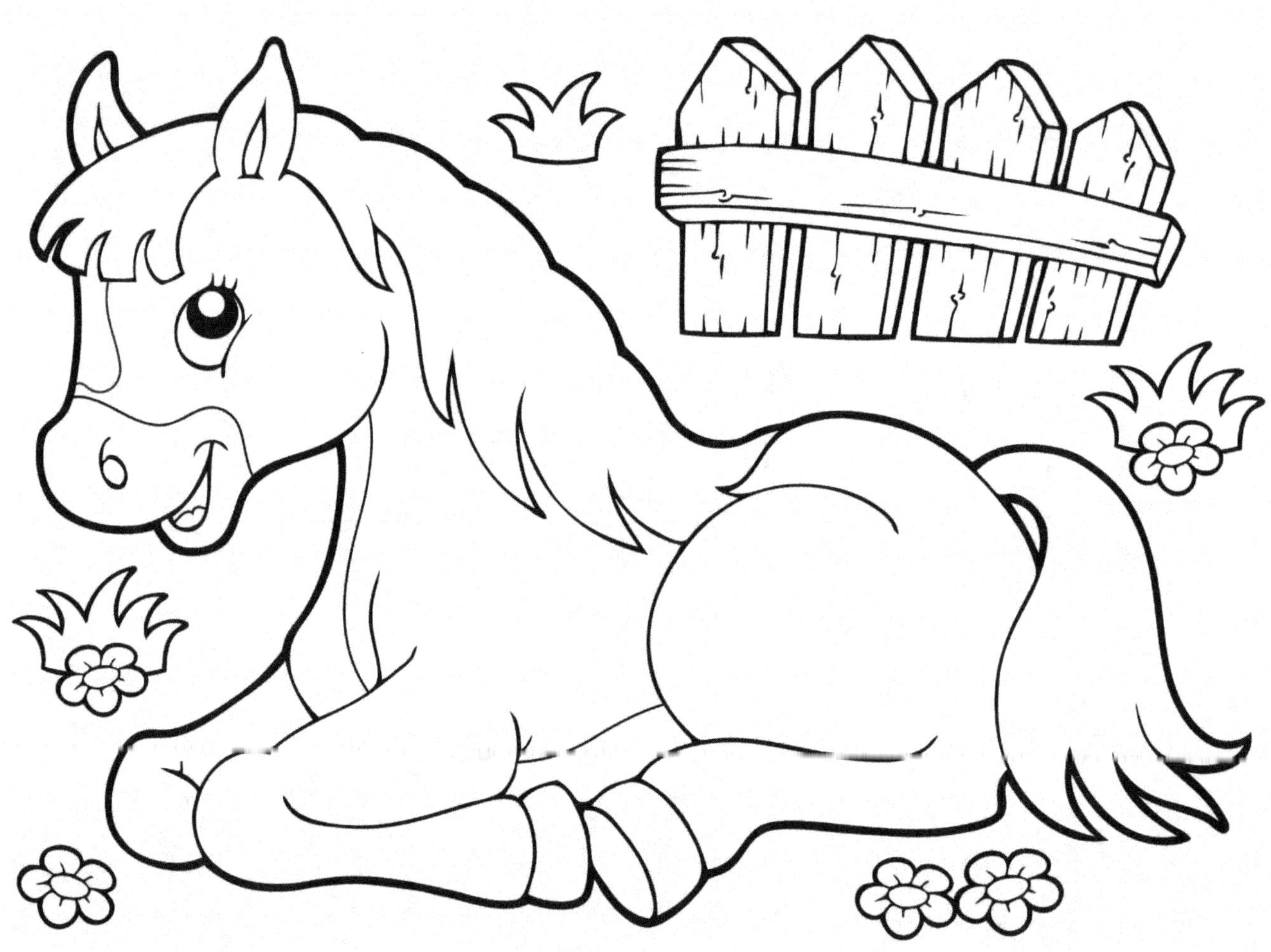

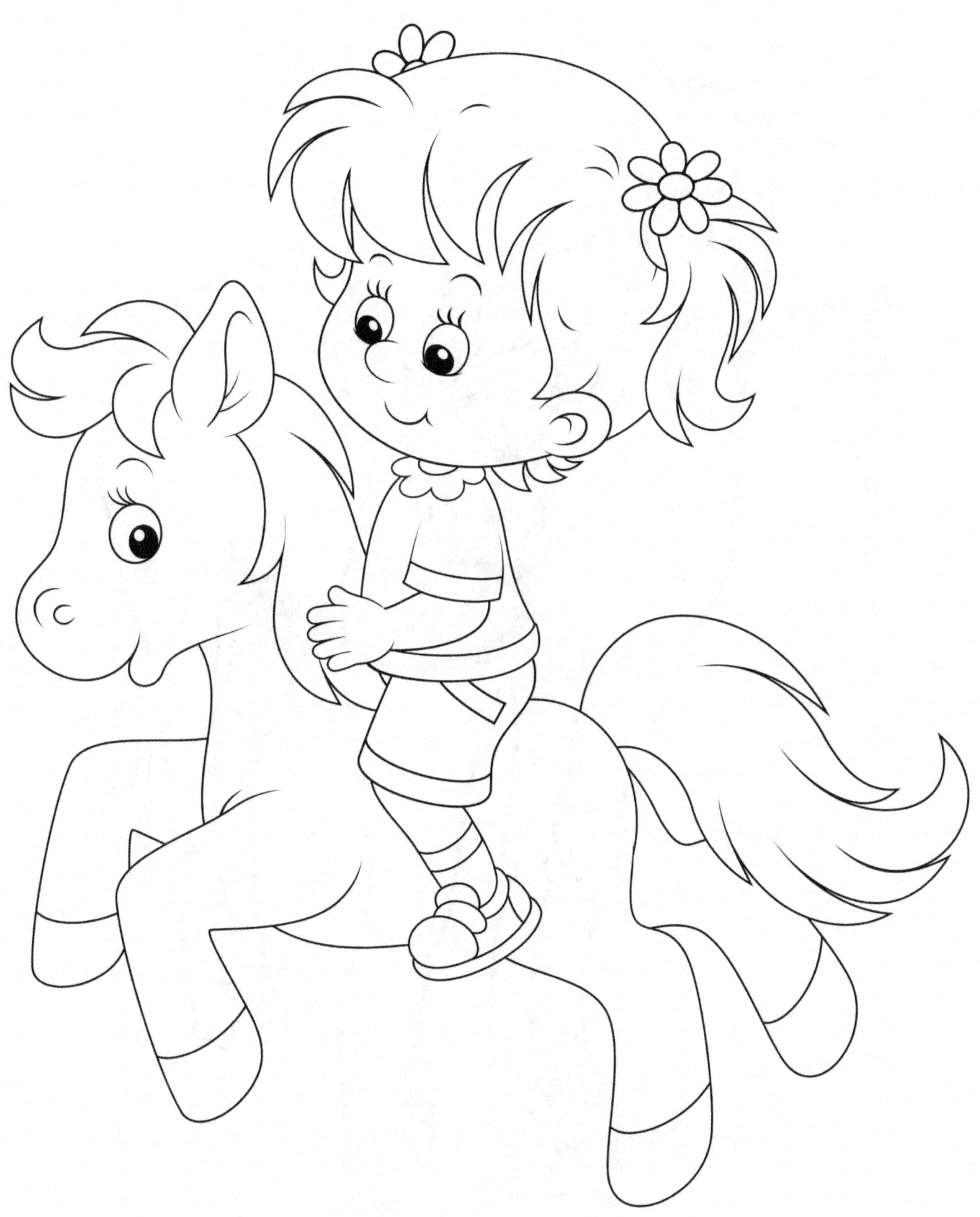

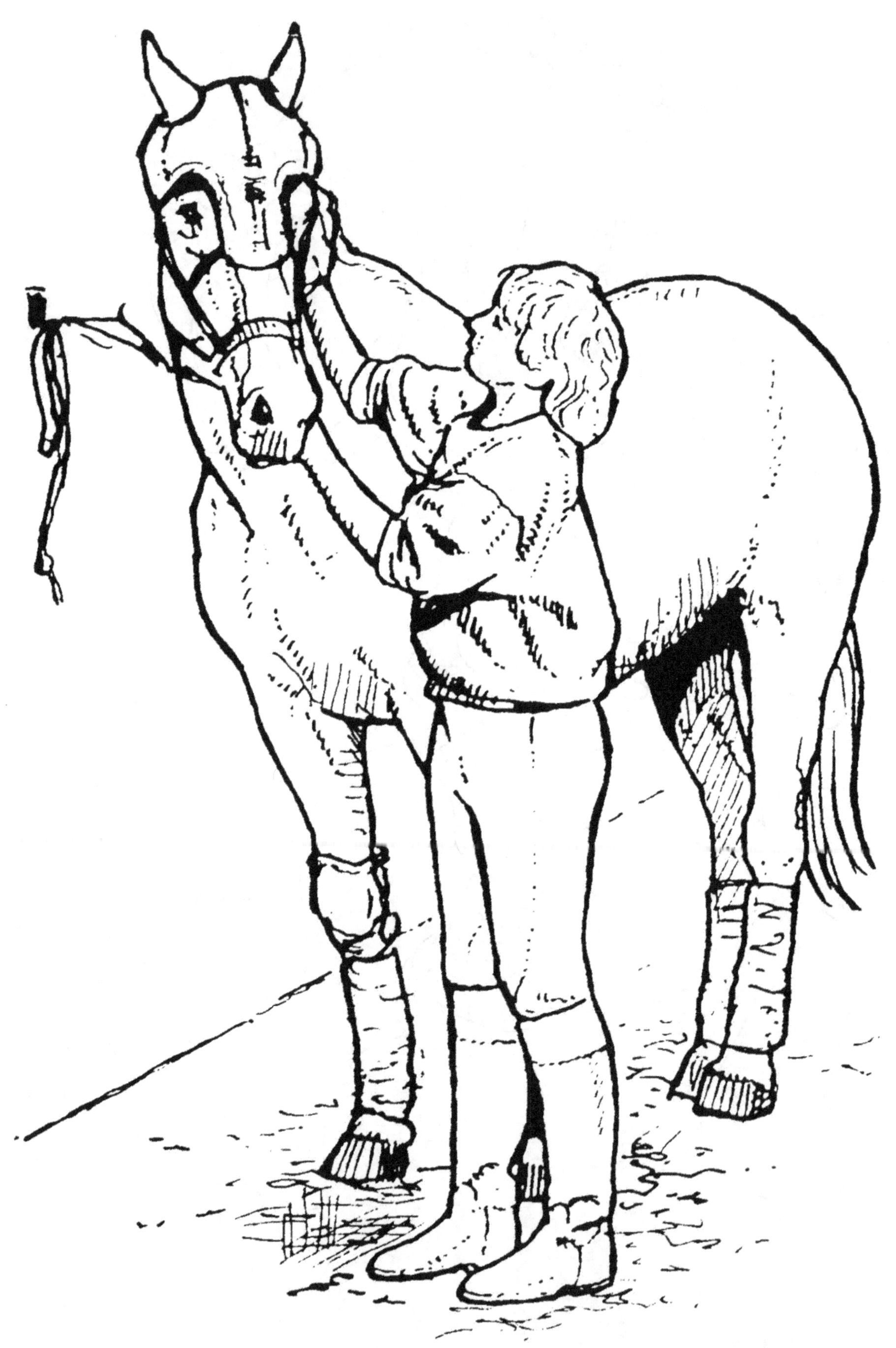

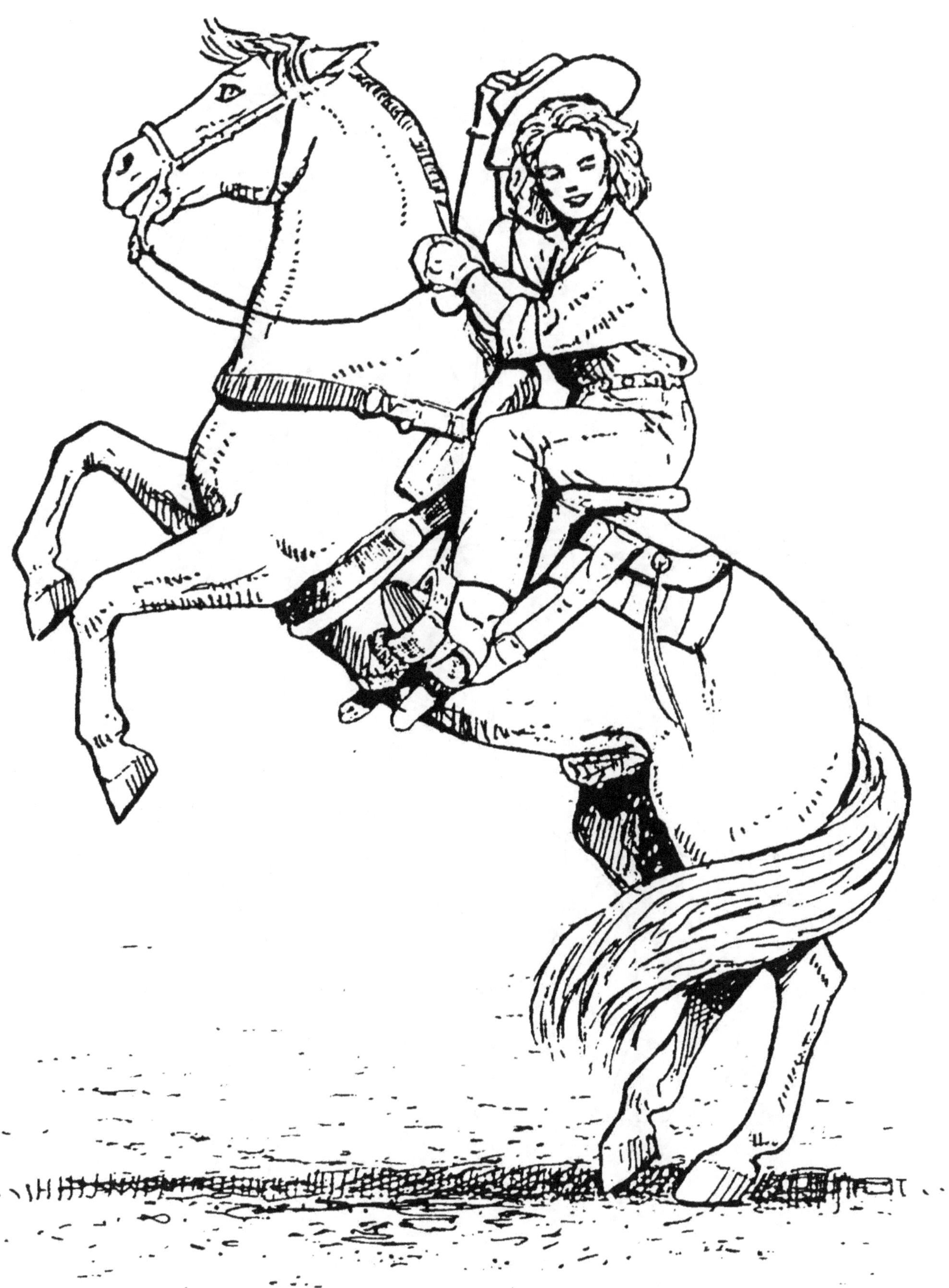

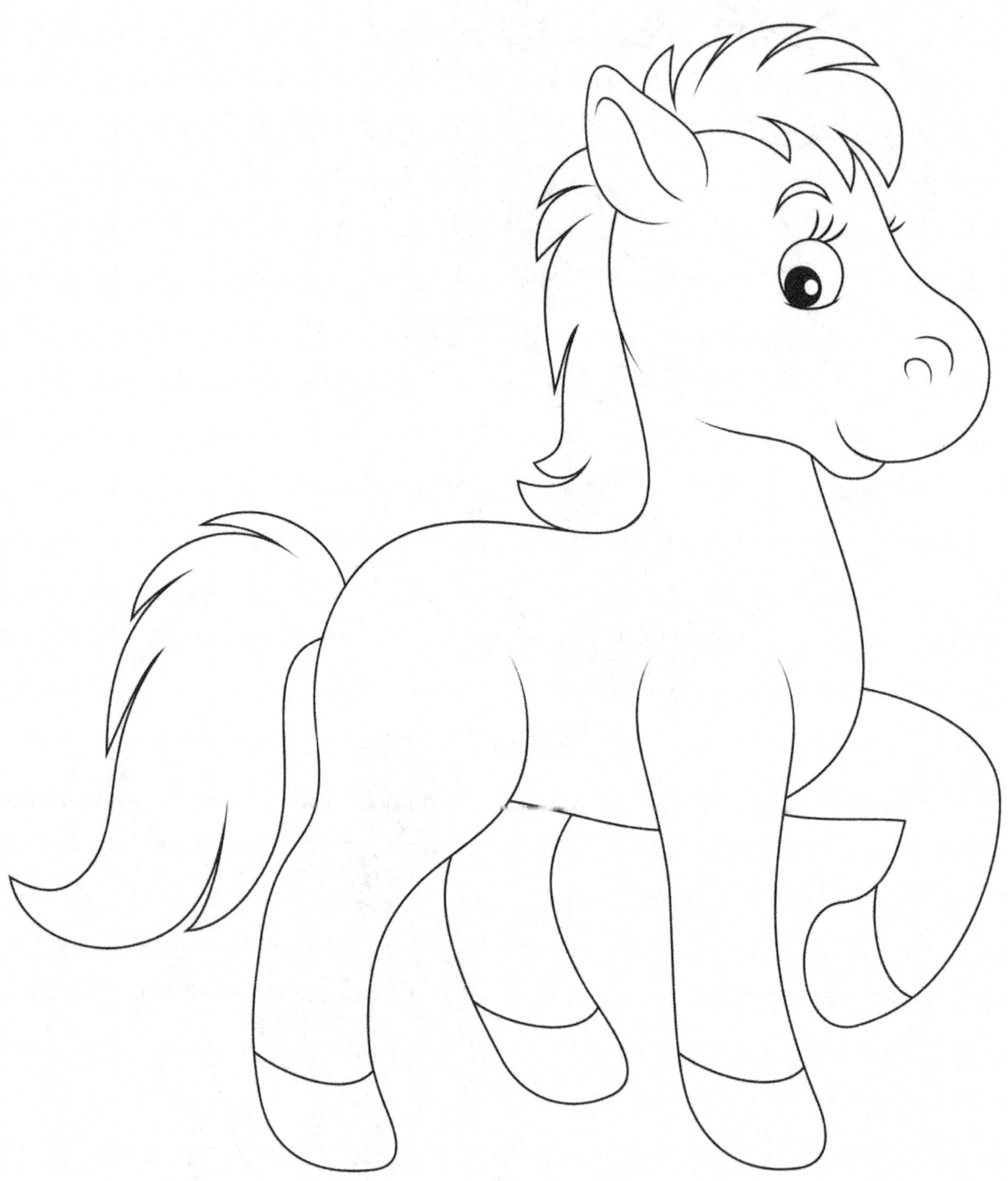

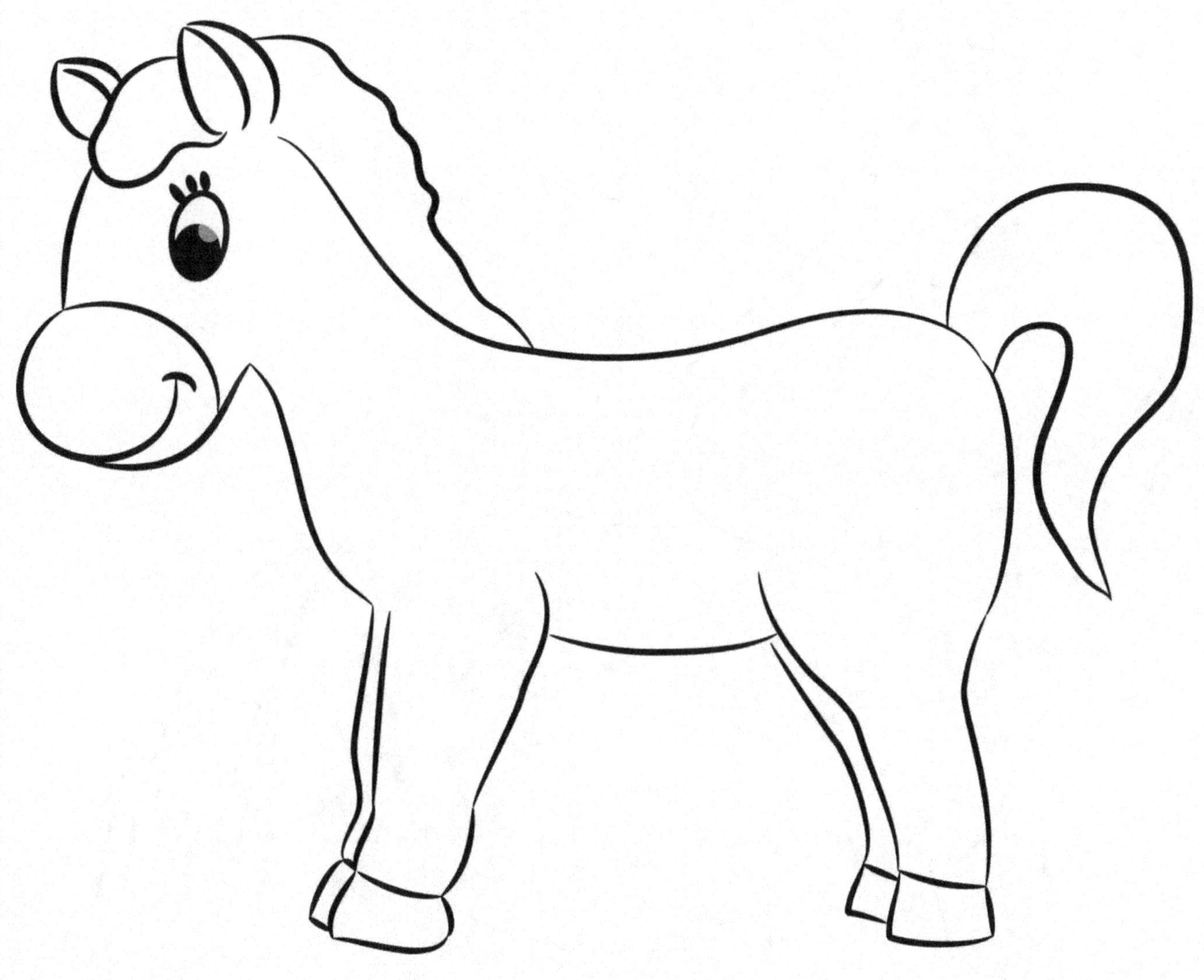

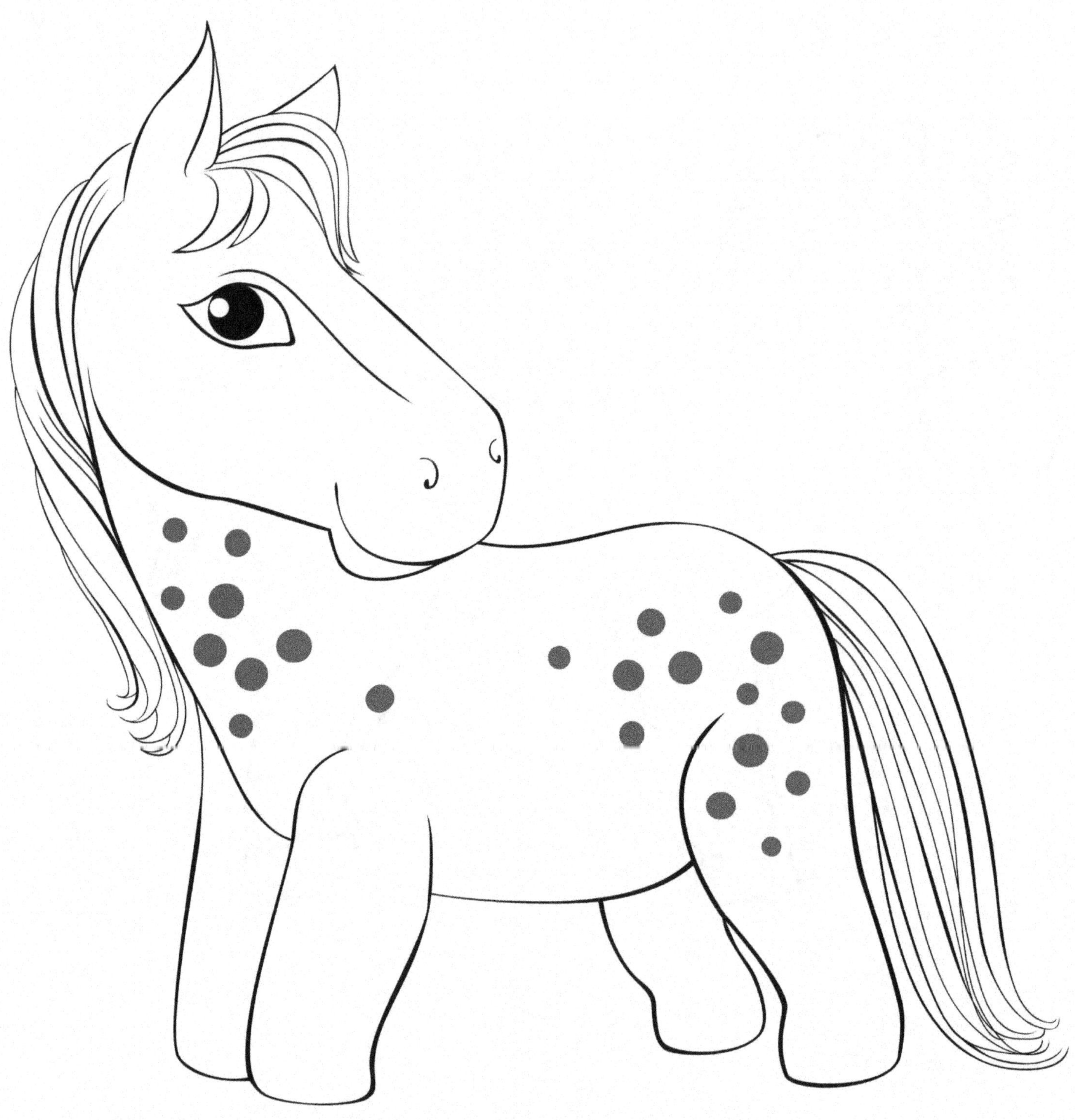

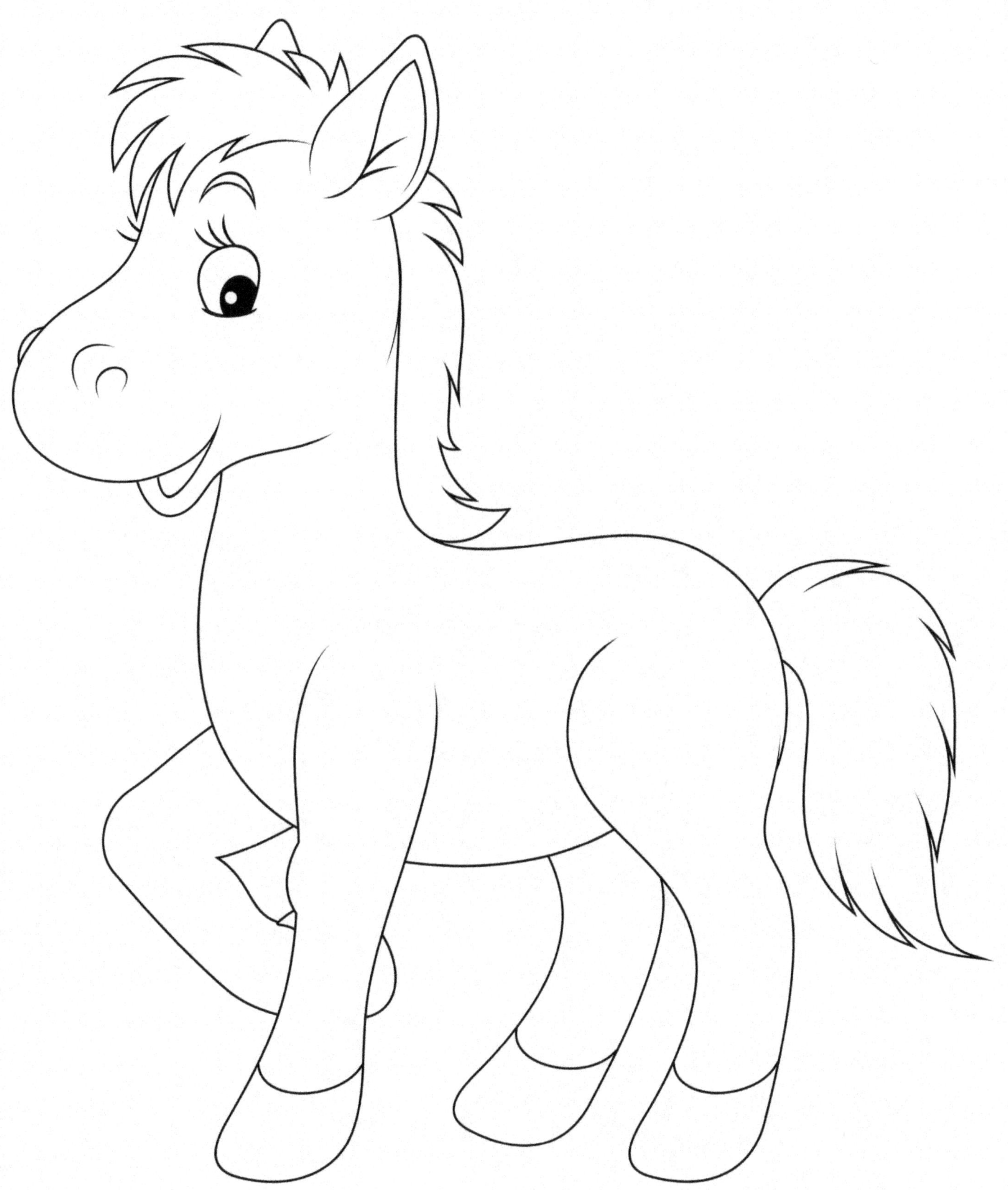

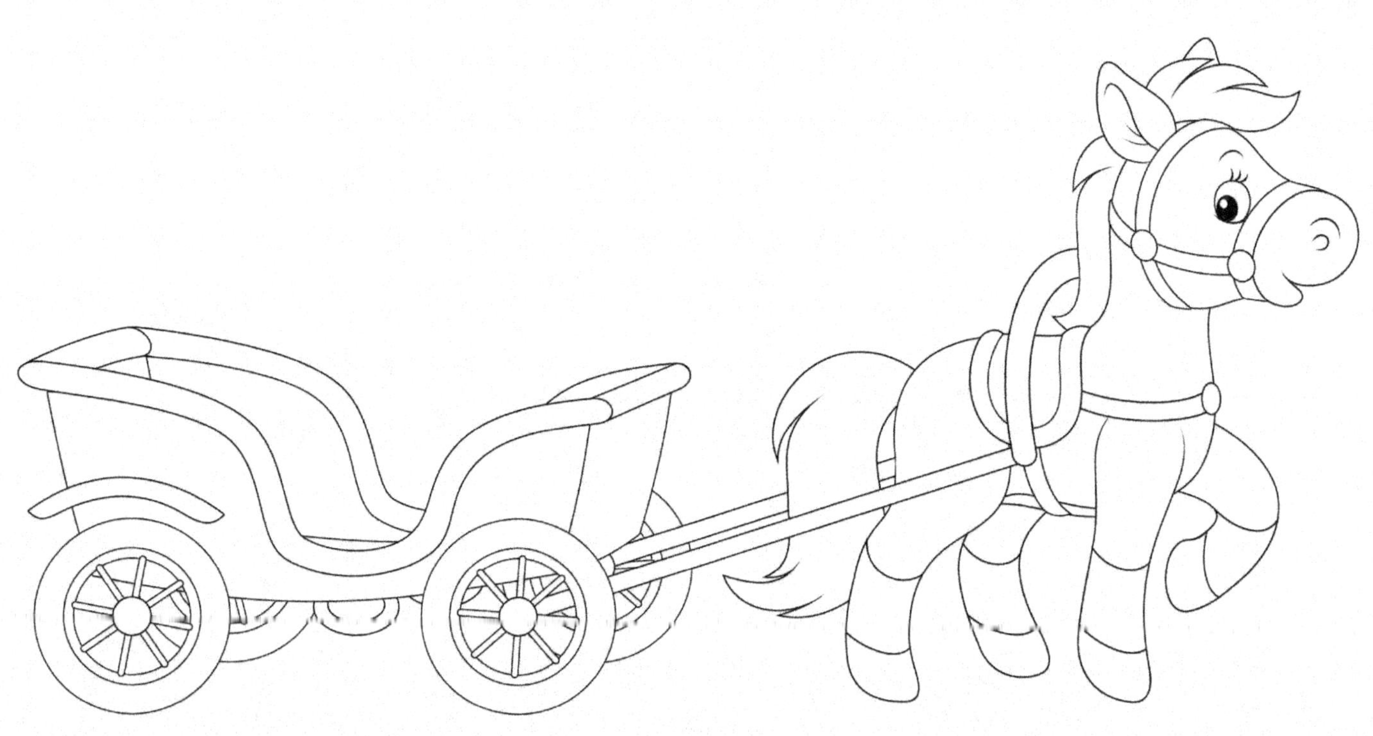

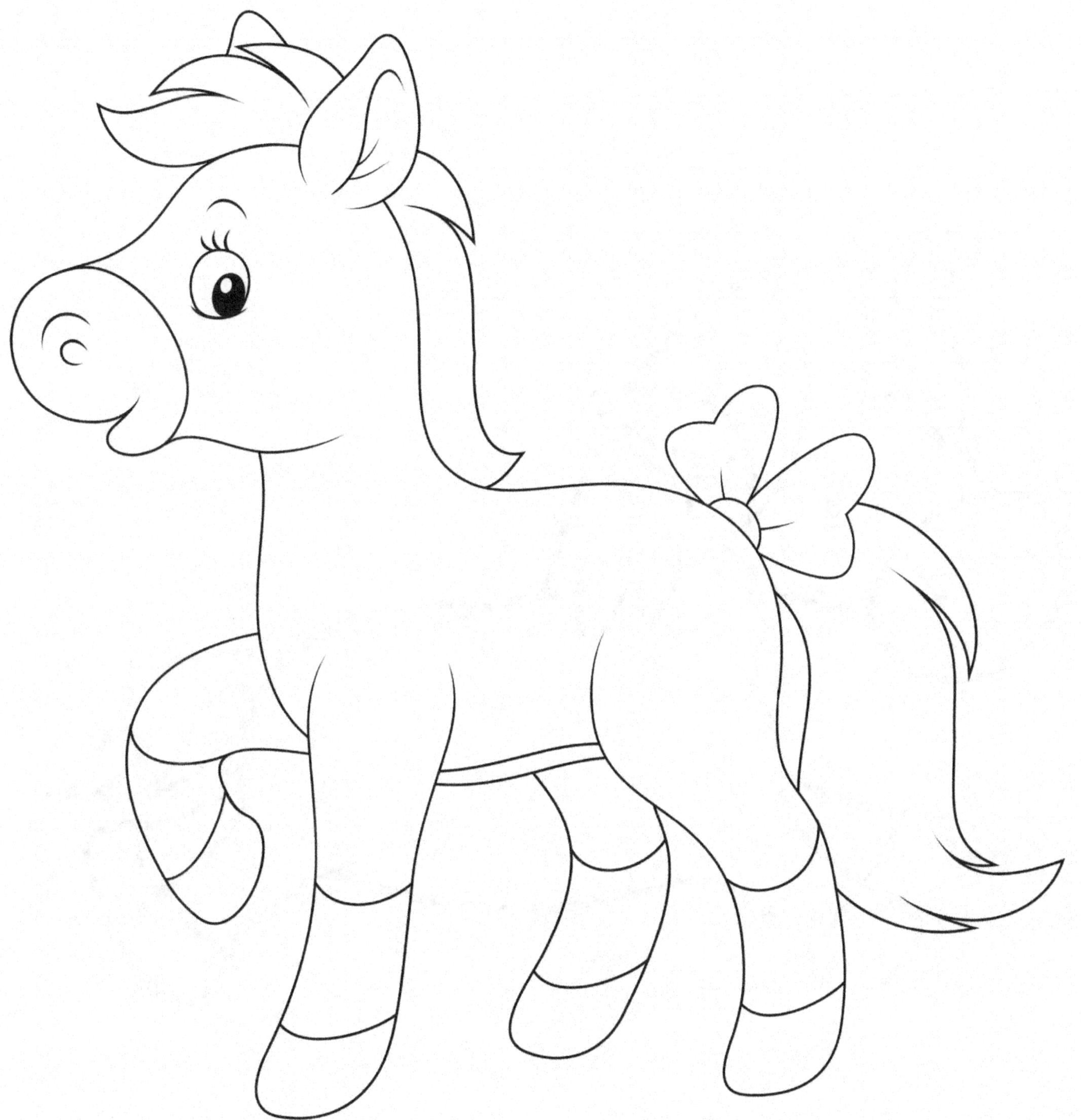

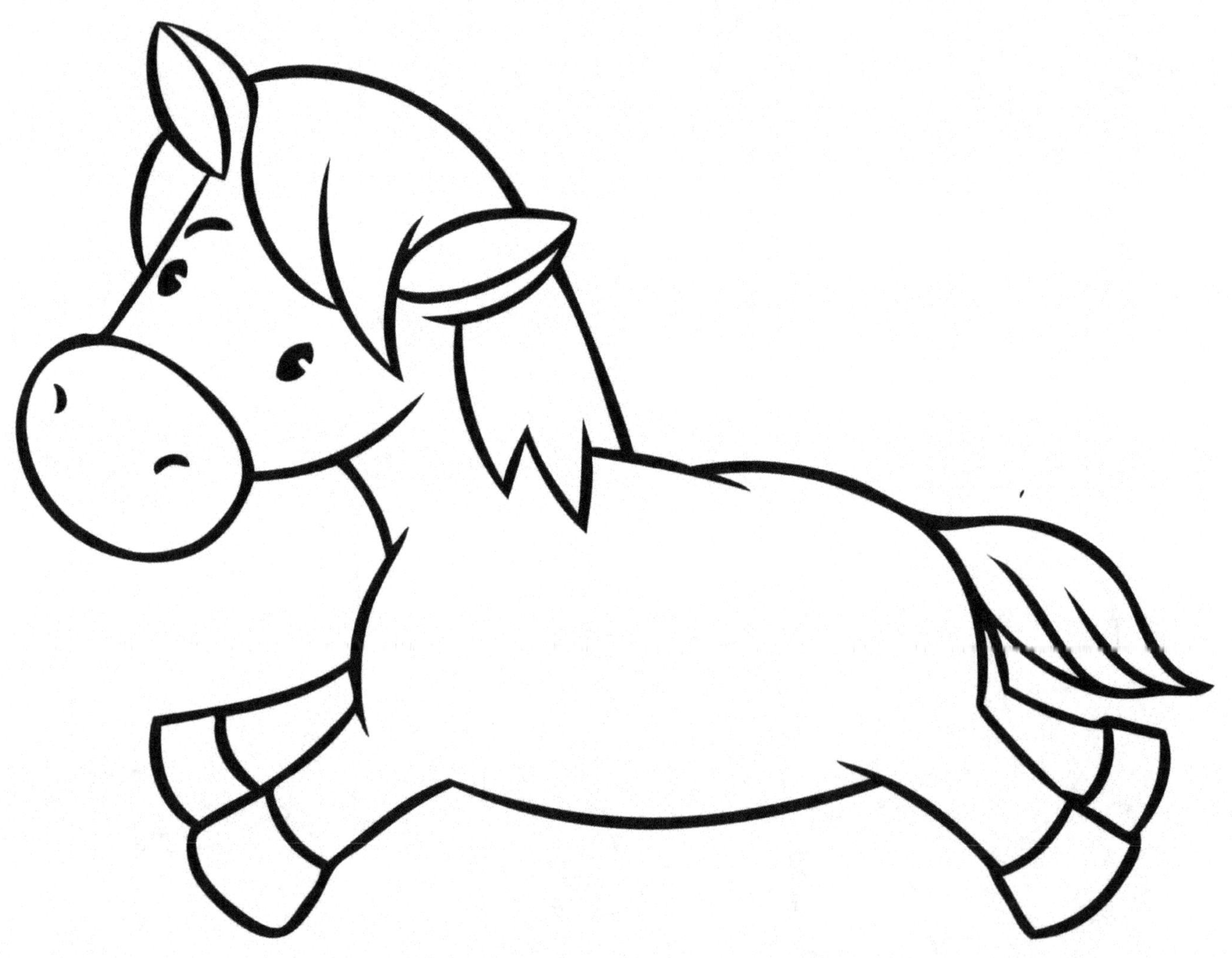

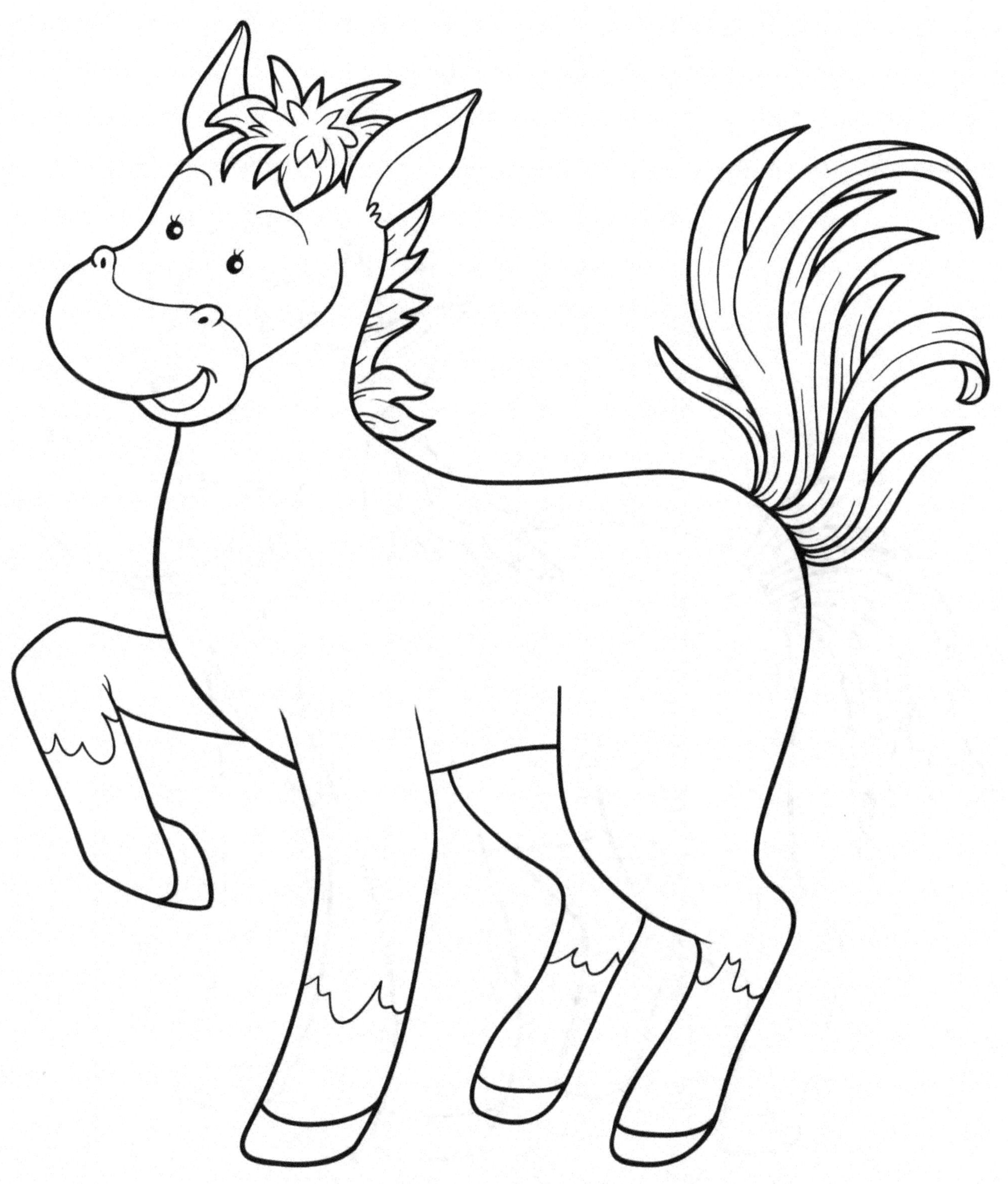

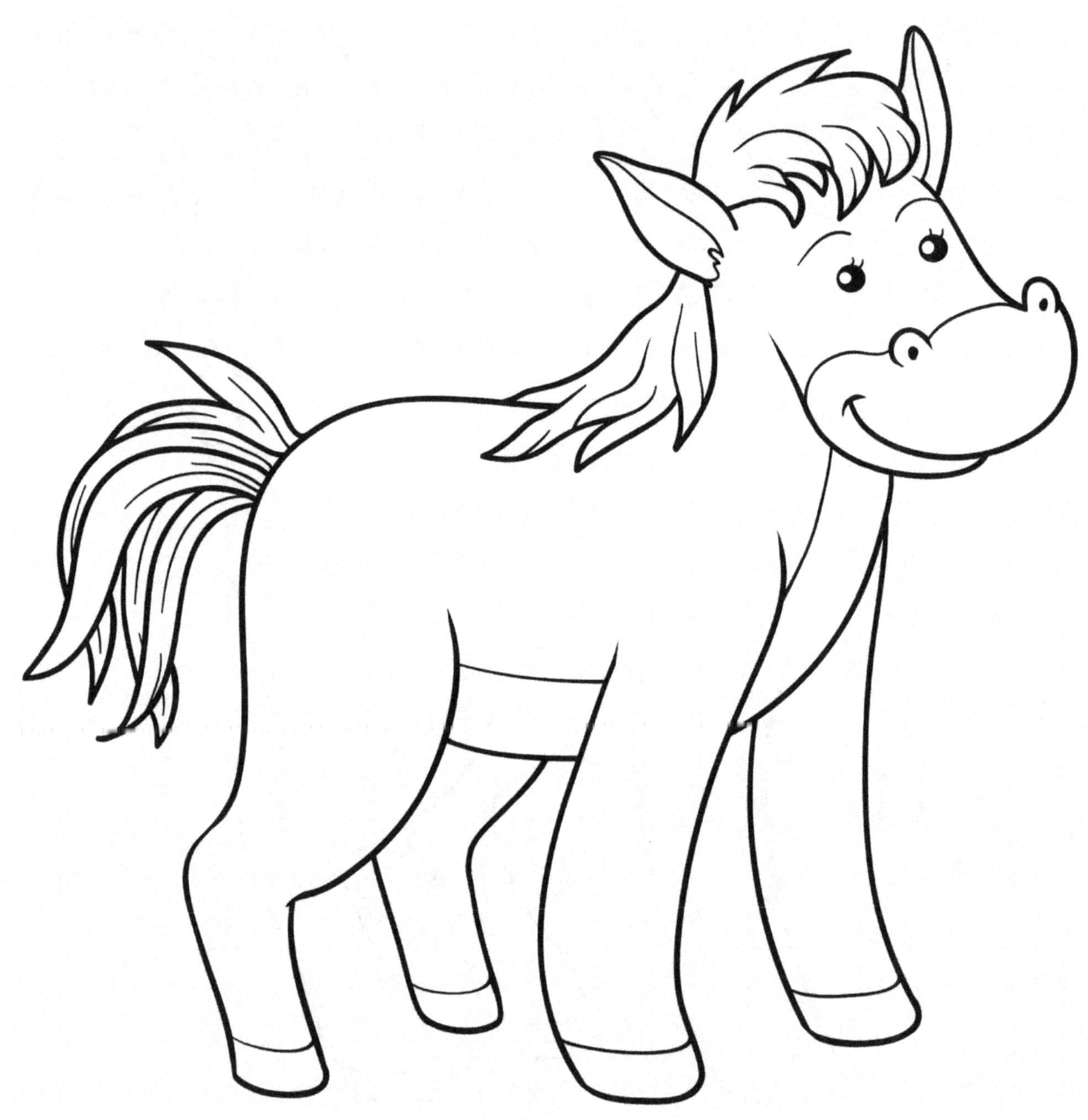

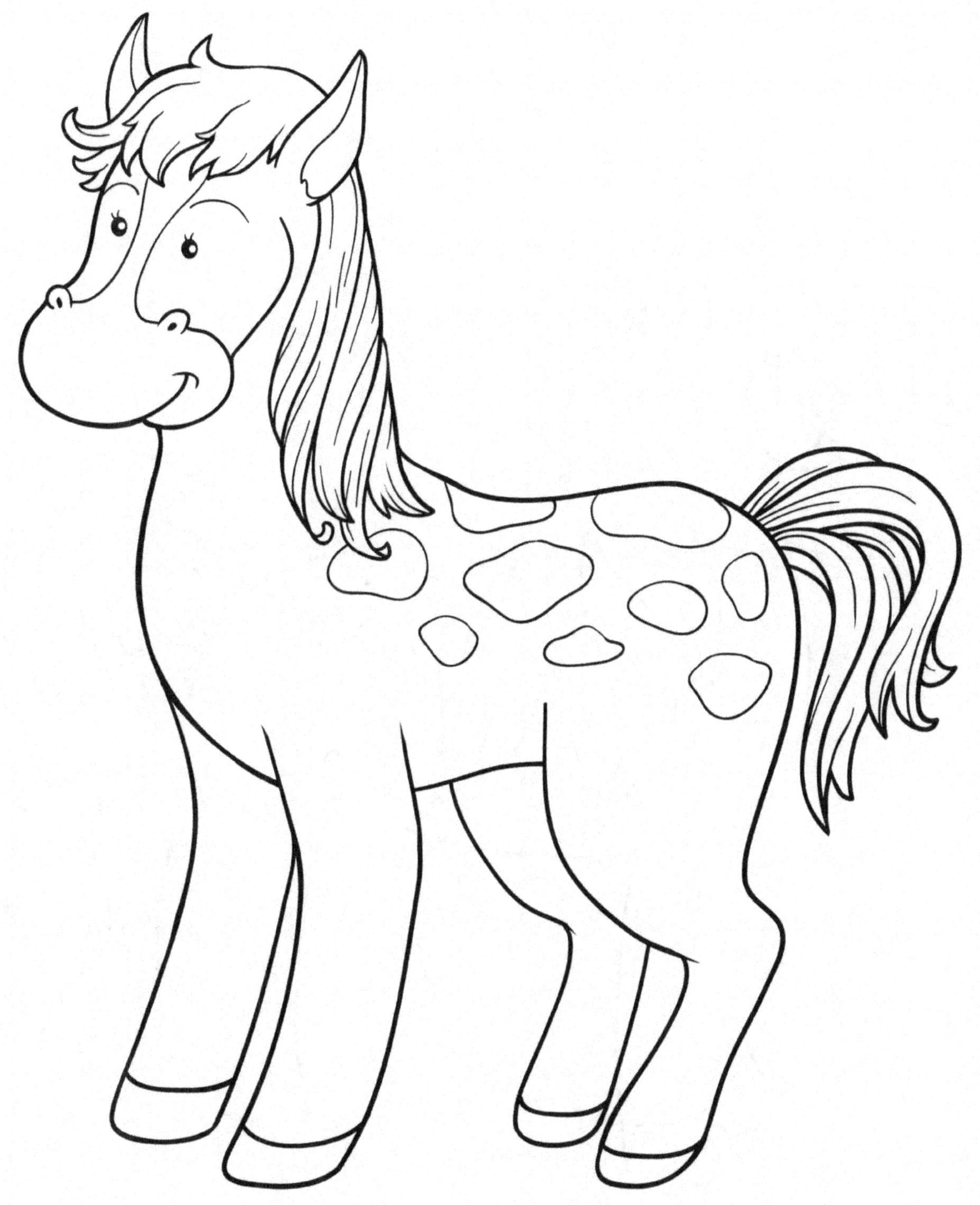

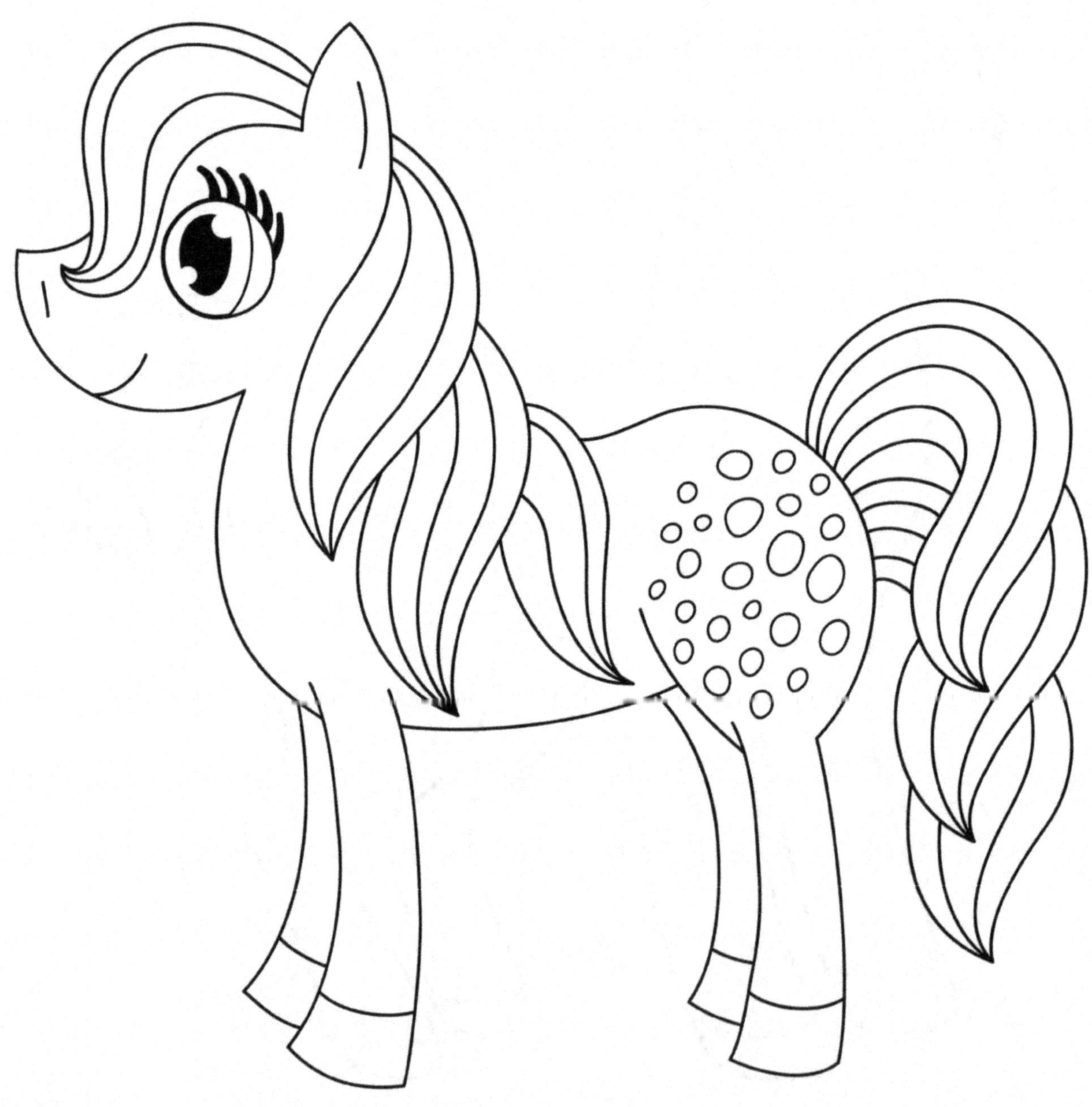

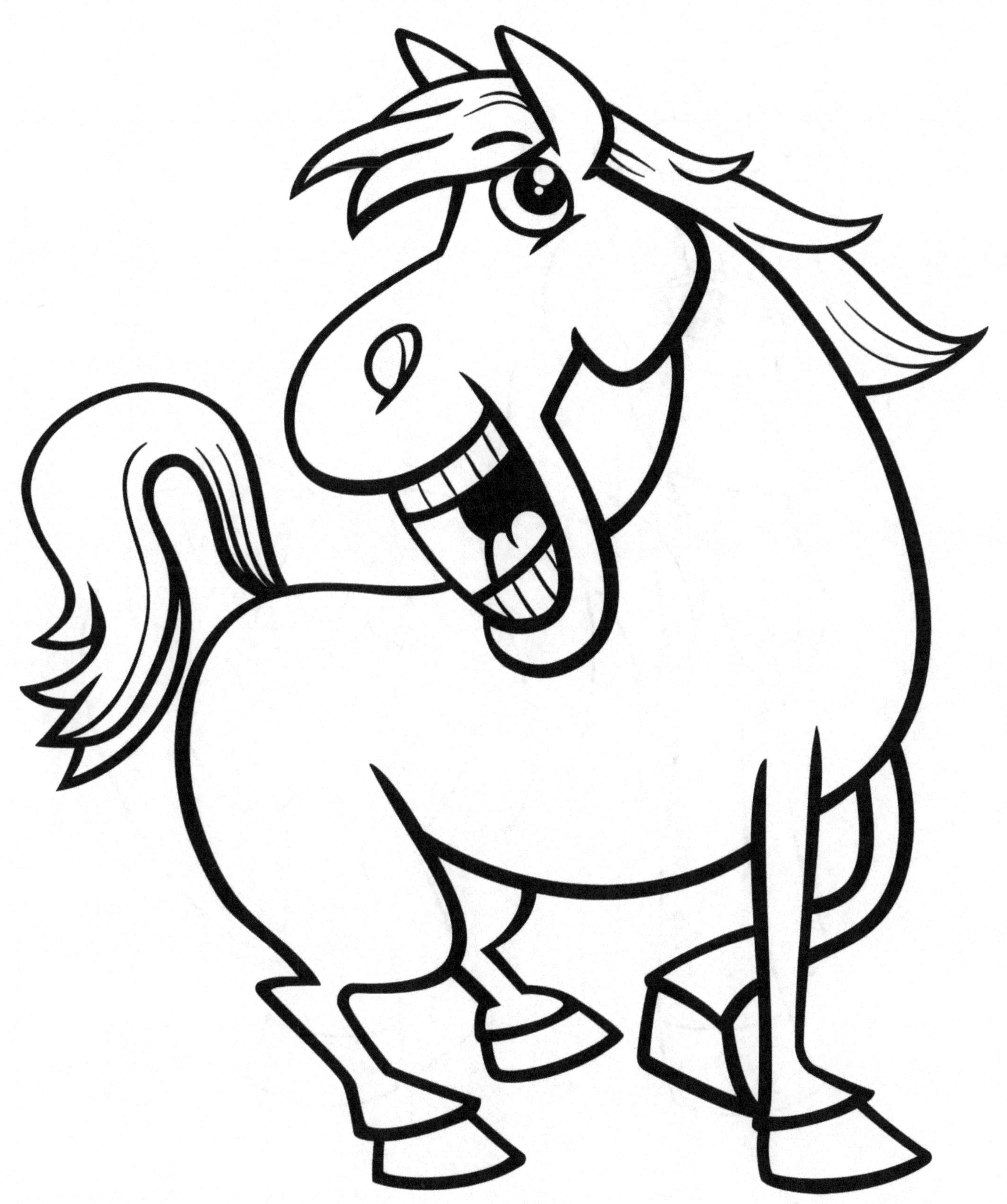

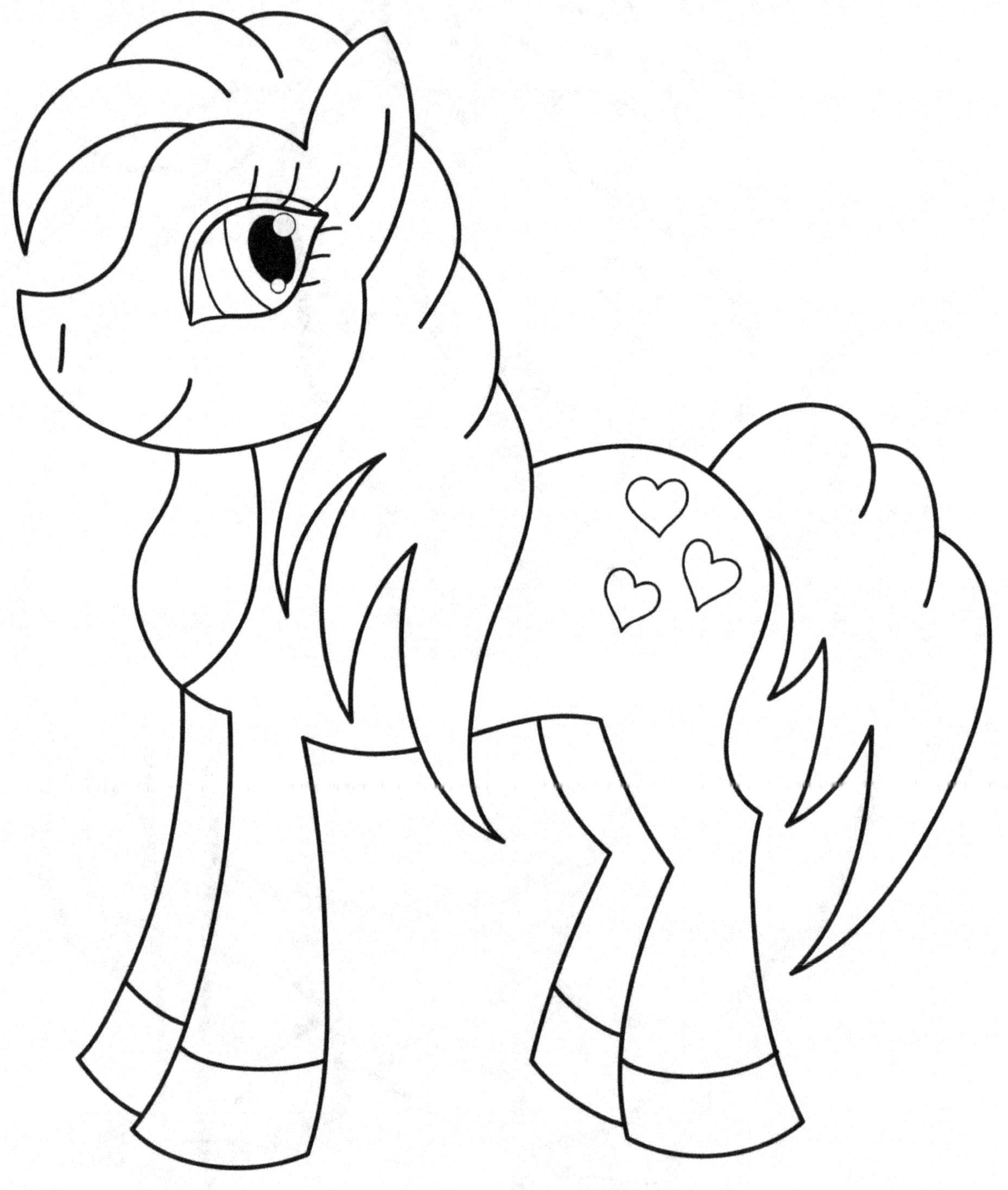

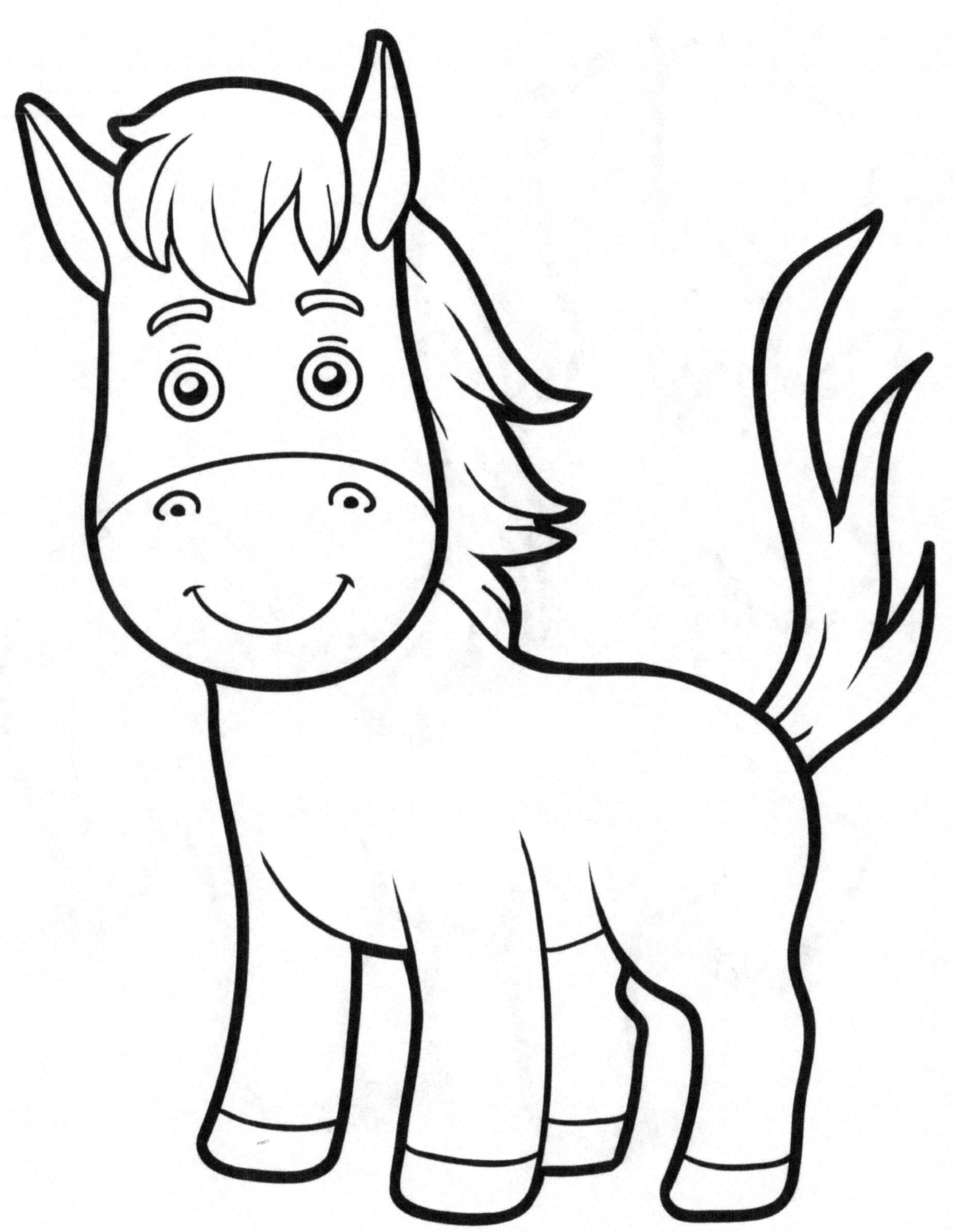

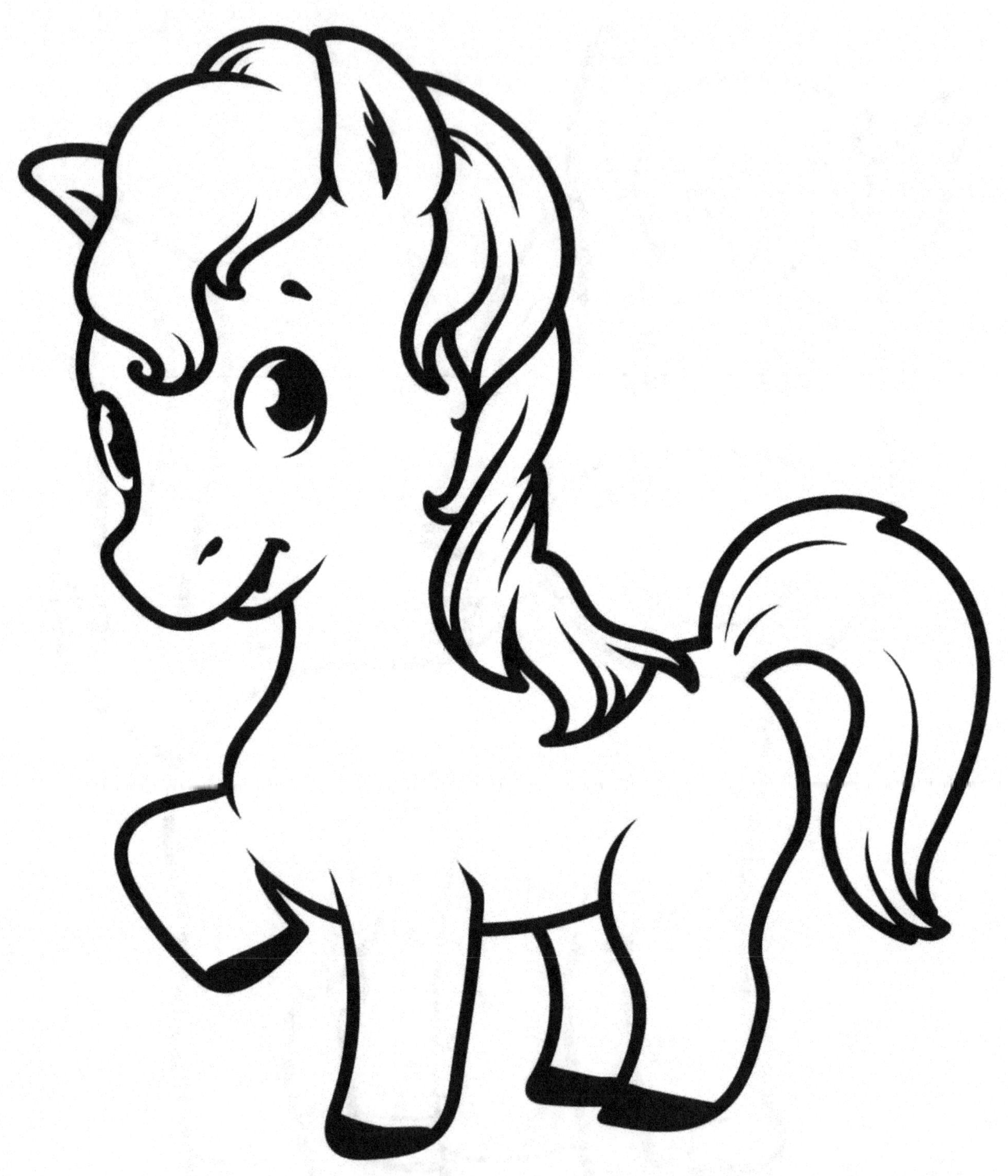

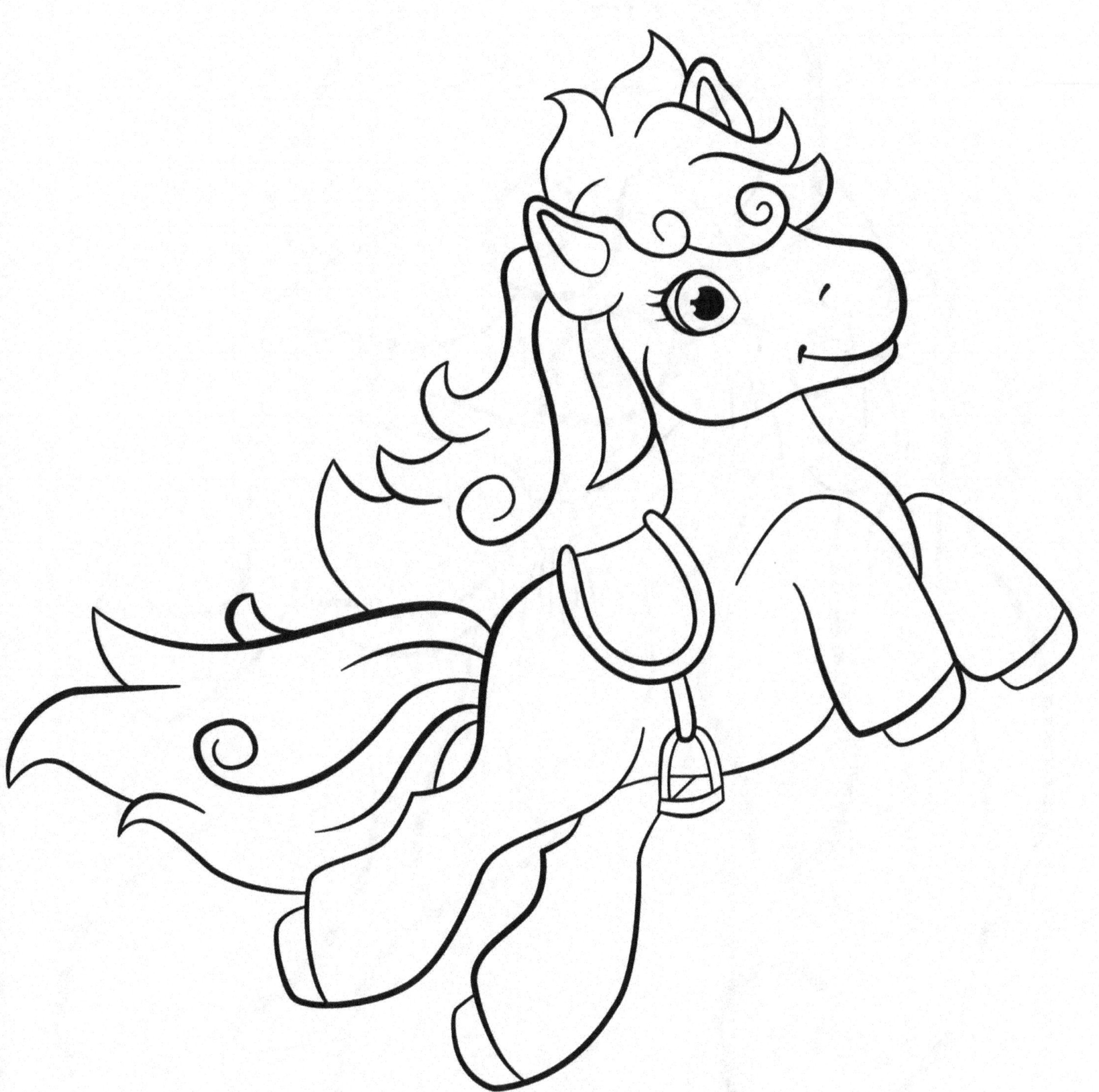

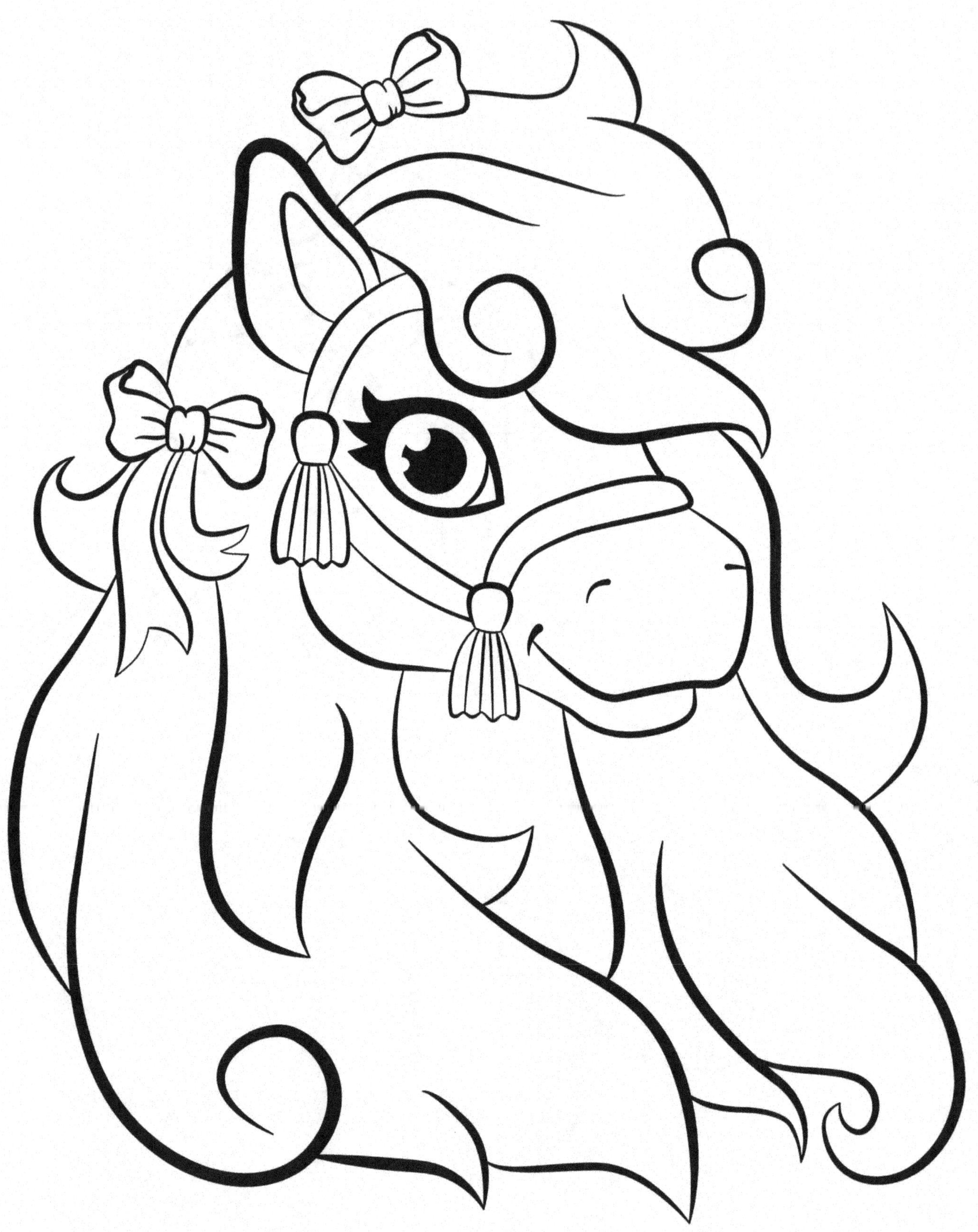

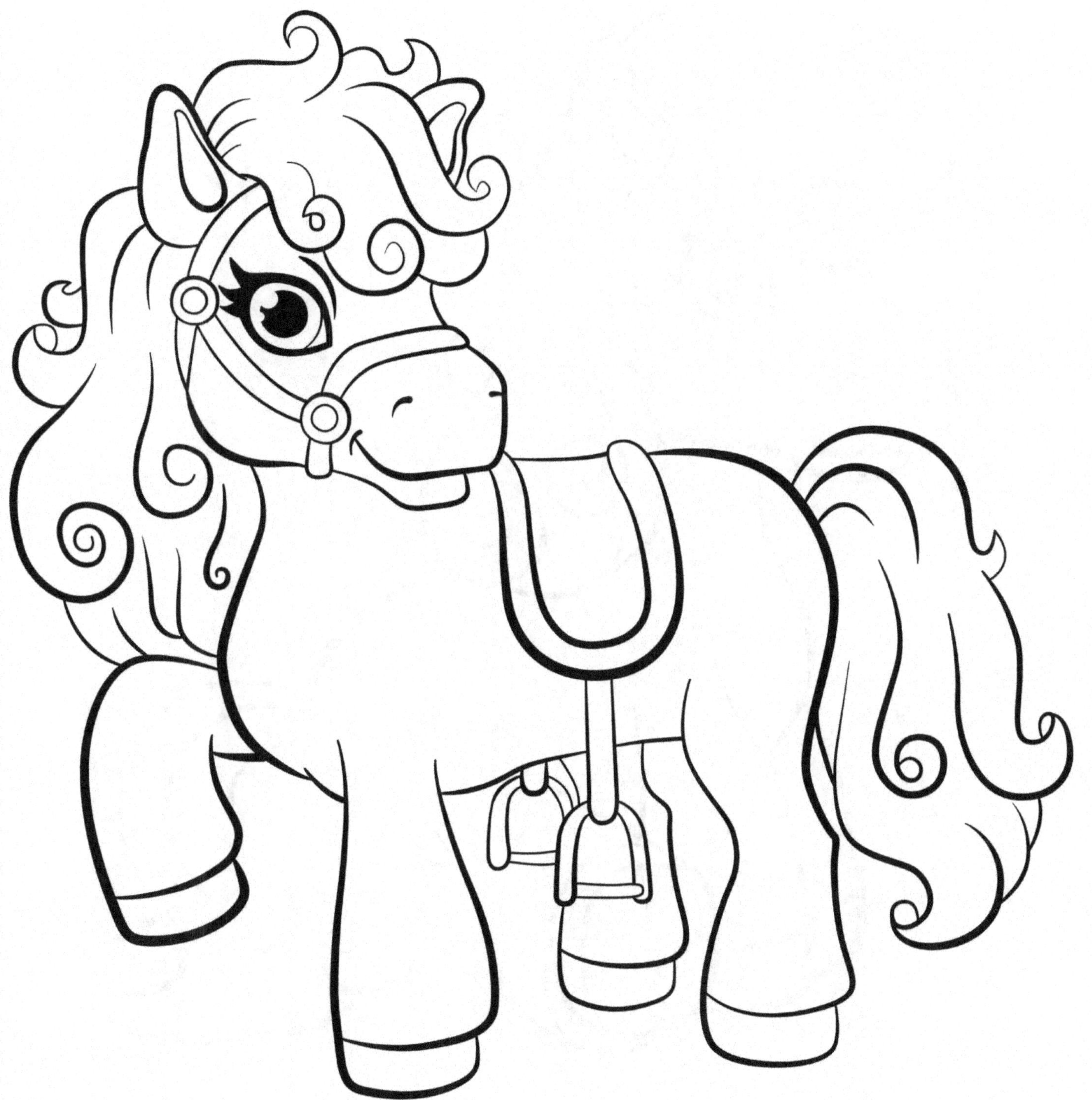

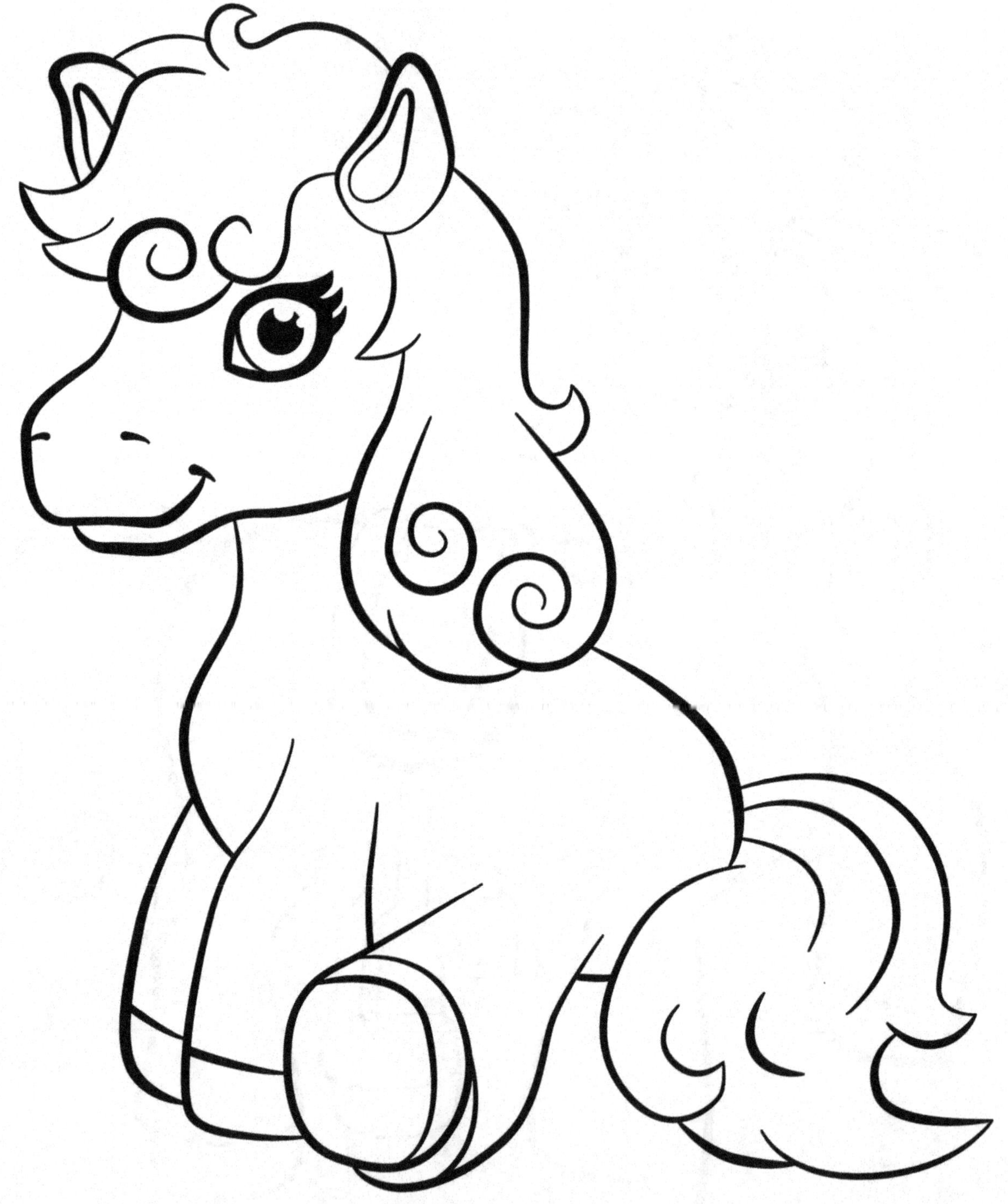

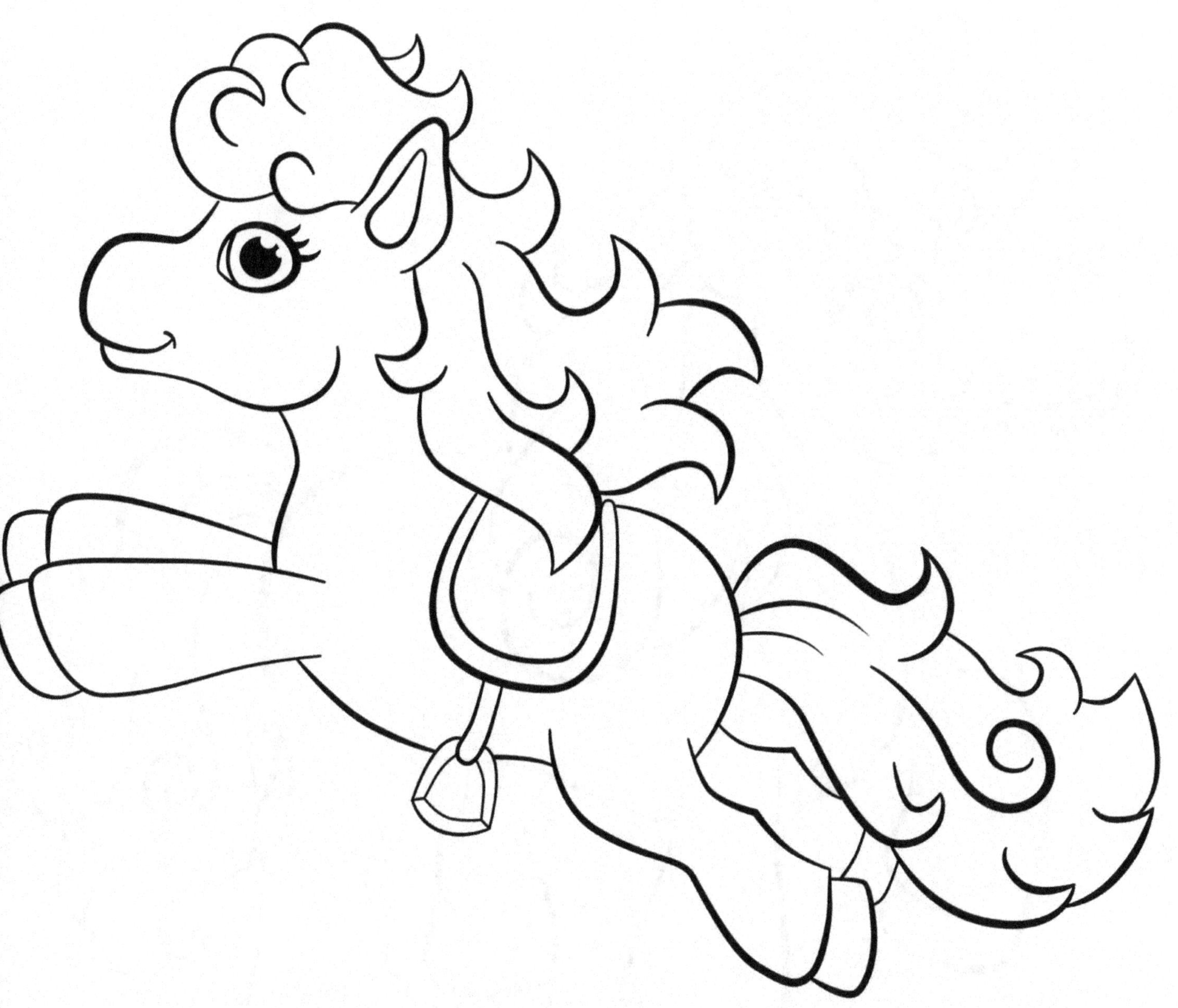

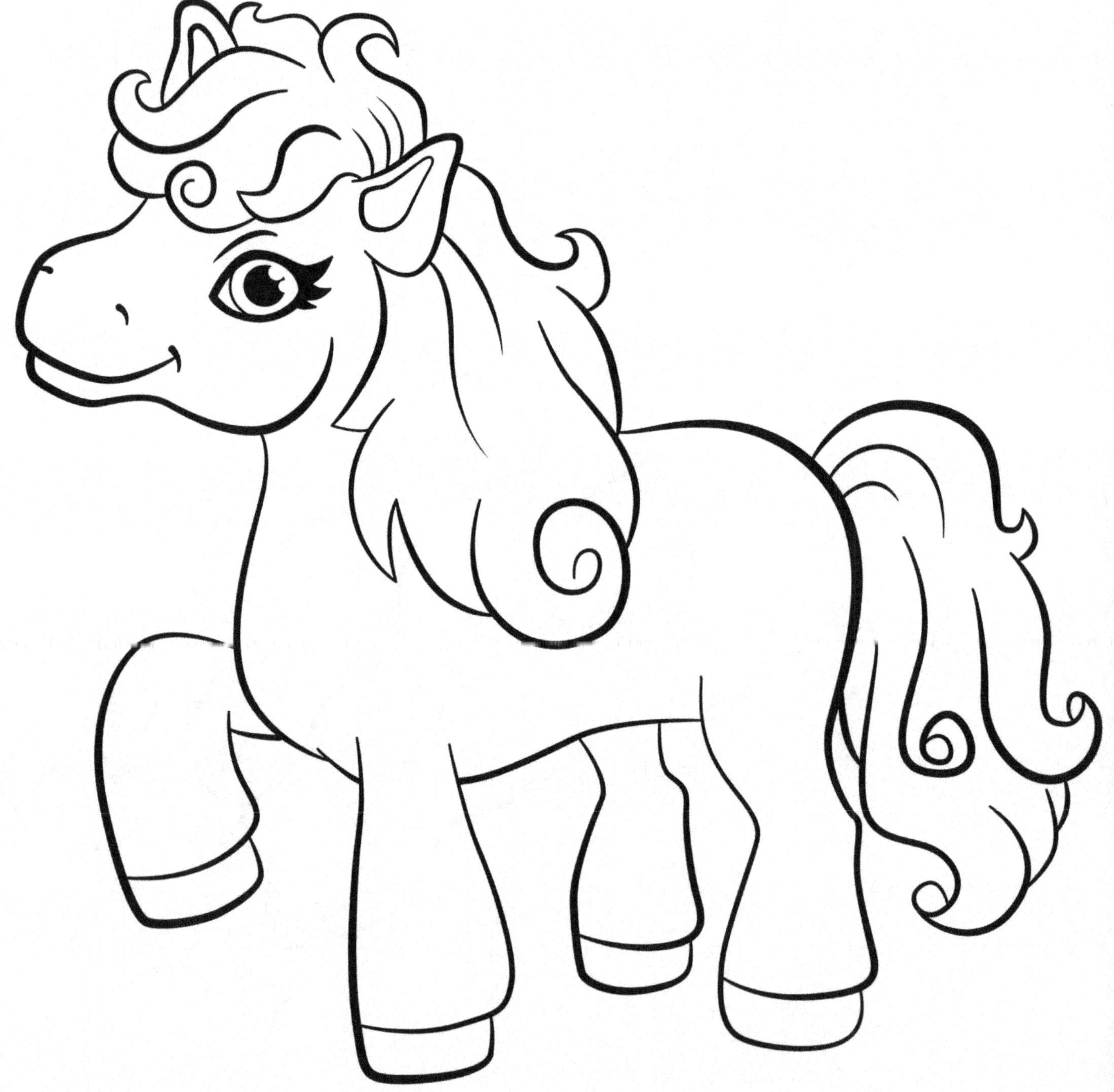

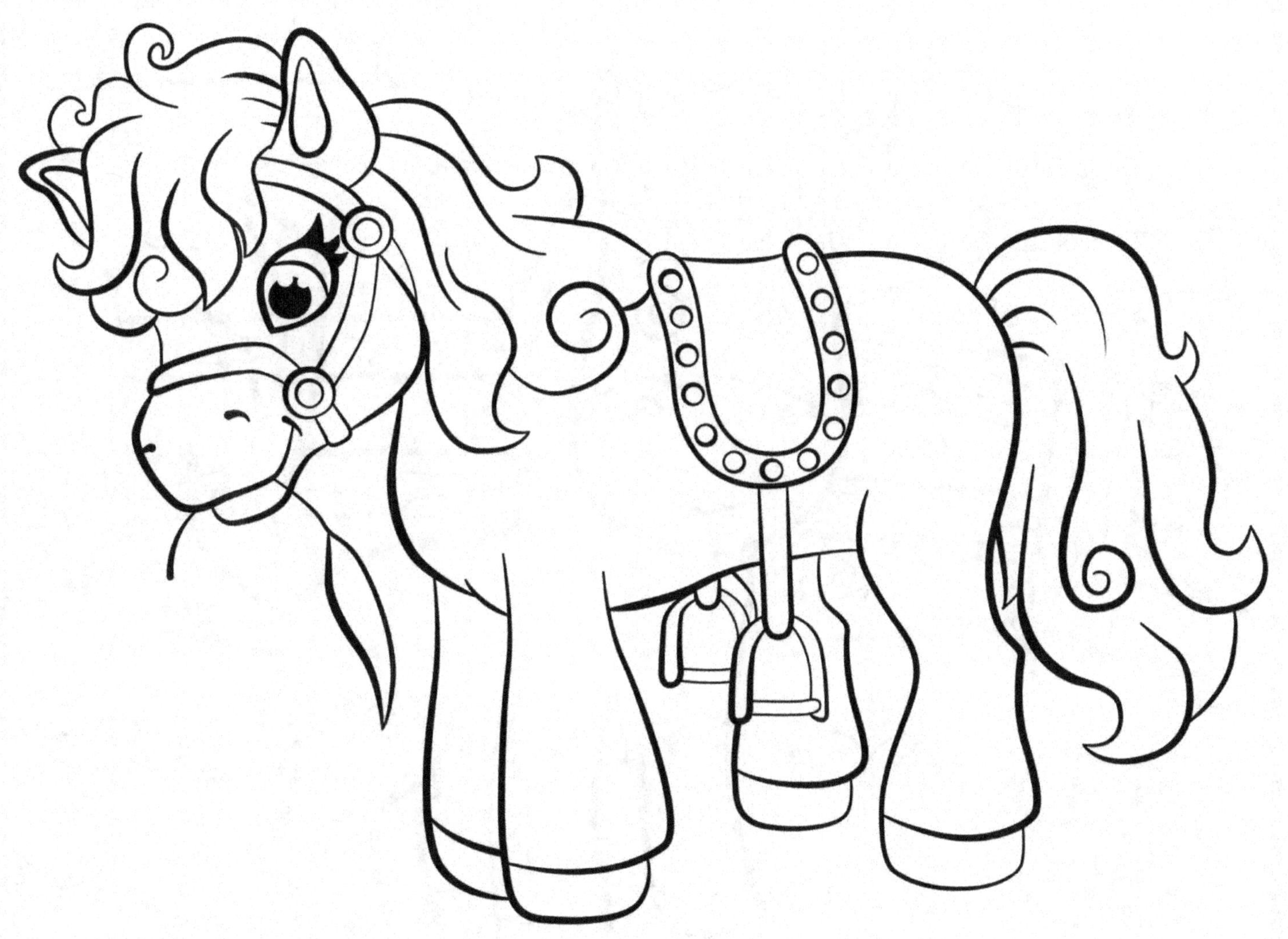

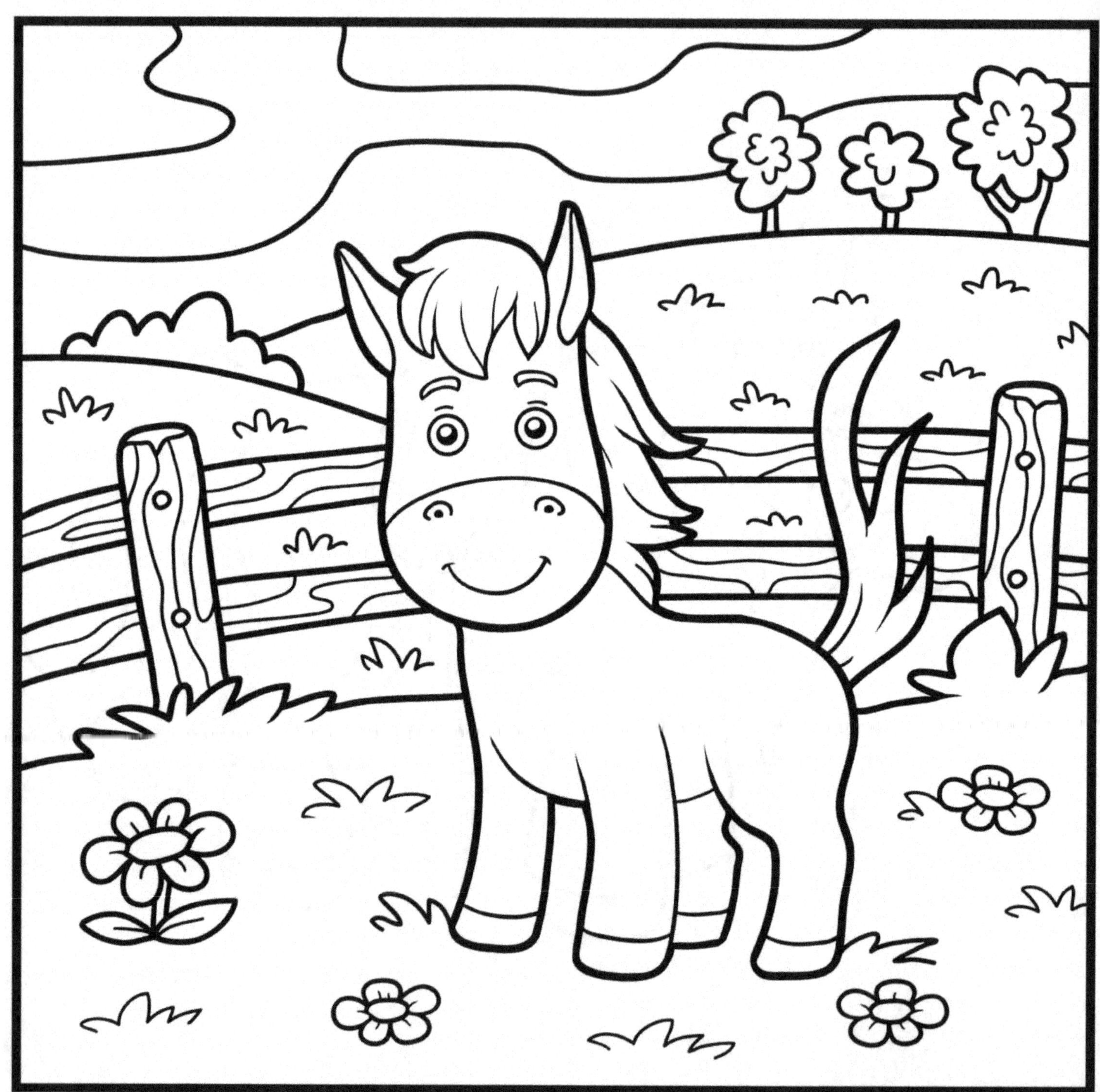